Comments from Readers

As the writing of *Improving Personal Effectiveness* progressed, a panel of more than sixty people read the entire manuscript. Their backgrounds cut across socioeconomic, educational, professional, and generational categories—students, younger people early in their careers, others who have gained some momentum in their careers, members of the clergy, seniors now active in new areas of life. These are some of their comments.

Really concise; this is a book you want to read about twice a year.
— WD, oil industry executive

TACT...*I wish I had read this ten years ago*
— DAC. vice president, advertising

All age groups stand to benefit from the food for thought fed by this book.
— SWF, economist

Each chapter is complete in itself...The reader can pick and choose where to concentrate.
— SA, optometrist

This would help some of my friends with MBA's who find themselves really stressed at their jobs because they had so little experience outside of school.
— MED, graduate student

Basic skills emanate from basic truths; there are basic truths in this book which can never be discarded. They are applicable on all levels of problem-solving — on all levels of decision-making — on all levels of management.
— CWF, PhD engineering management

Quotations...spark interest and mobilize thinking. Examples derived from a variety of sources appeal to a wide range of readers...Loved the annotated bibliography!
— VGD, school nurse

So much content here...information in every paragraph, could have great discussions on each one of them.
— JDL, private investor

I was underlining significant points, but found myself underlining everything. It is so thought-provoking...a book for everyone!
— JCL, homemaker

Many people can benefit from learning to believe in themselves and others.
— EMF, self-employed

PERSONAL ETHICS...*this book takes us far beyond legal Code requirements.*
— DMcE, attorney

INTERCOMMUNICATION...LISTENING...*I saw how this can really work at an important meeting this week. I made myself listen to what everyone had to say and then I didn't have to say much to have a real impact on the outcome of the meeting.* — DM, marketing executive

Since I became a widow I have had to make many adjustments in my life and manage things as I never did while my dear husband was alive. You can't imagine how helpful and encouraging this book has been!
— VVW, homemaker

We envision the book aimed at young adults (age frame 35 to 45) who have a credible track record in business to this point. They would be positioning themselves to move to a higher level. Our own children are enthusiastic. — EFM/JJM, retired educator/executive

I was particularly pleased with the "efficiency" of the writing.
— RAS, dean, engineering

PERSUASIVENESS...*I realize now that the hardest job I had in facilitating an early intervention special education program was persuading the parents that their children needed this help. I never looked at it this way until I read this chapter.* — DPB, early childhood teacher

IMPROVING PERSONAL EFFECTIVENESS *has very broad possibilities for people who have positions in which communication is paramount...I could see myself using it in workshops for business people, school counselors, sales personnel, etc..* — VTA, PhD, communication

Young people often go into a job full of enthusiasm but with little knowledge about how to convince another person about an idea or a product. I felt your suggestions were good common sense. I am sharing this with my son. I know it will be helpful. — CM, member church council

Objectivity...*the truth is that nothing must succeed in concealing the truth.*
— WFW, retired chaplain, US Army

As a test, I asked our marketing director for his reaction to the ideas. His response was that there is a basis here for seminar discussions for professionals and business courses in continuing education programs.
— DBS, corporate director

Clearly, the ideas in this book have worked for the author for nearly a century...these are standards of personal conduct that have been forwarded for centuries, transcend history and still function in today's society.
— BD, PhD, philosophy

Great ideas... no over-elaboration... saves reading time.
— MJD, physician.

IMPROVING
PERSONAL EFFECTIVENESS

PUBLISHING

Memo from a Modern Methuselah

IMPROVING
PERSONAL EFFECTIVENESS

George W. Fotis

Edited by Betty Persico Fotis

A Practical Guide
to Nine
Powerful
People-Skills

Career/Scope
PUBLISHING

Improving Personal Effectiveness: *A Practical Guide to 9 Powerful People-Skills* is available at special discounts when ordered in bulk quantities (5 or more copies per order).

Write: *Career/Scope Publishing*
8987-309 E. Tanque Verde Road, Suite 326
Tucson, Arizona 85749-9399

Call: (800) 256-3842

This book is designed to share with the reader insights gained by the author in dealing with other people. It is sold with the understanding that the publisher is not engaged in rendering professional advice or services. If further information or other expert assistance is required, professional services should be sought.

Library of Congress Information
Publisher's Cataloging-in-Publication Data
(Prepared by Quality Books, Inc.)

Fotis, George W.
        Improving personal effectiveness : a practical guide to 9 powerful people-skills/George W. Fotis ; edited by Betty Persico Fotis
        p. cm. -- (Memo from a modern Methuselah)
        Includes bibliographical references.
        ISBN 0-9648471-0-8
        Preassigned LCCN: 95-61423

        1. Conduct of life. 2. Success. 3. Self-actualization. I. Title.

BJ1611.F68 1995   158.1
                           QB195-204599

To Betty

*All human activities
aim at some good.*

—ARISTOTLE

Acknowledgments

THIS IS TO ACKNOWLEDGE WITH GRATEFUL THANKS the many friends, family members, and acquaintances whose comments and assistance were of great value in helping to keep this project on track. I hope I have included all of them here. Sometimes just a "thumbs up" was enough to make a difference.

Many thanks are due to the family members and friends who served as a panel of advisers: Maria and Peter Arabia, Barbara and Edward Ball, Bernice and Al Bender, Donald Blair, Lorraine and George Davis, Rev. Jerry Elrod, Sharon Elrod, Brian, Marla and Marisa Domino, Valerie and George Domino, Donna Dunham, Eleanor Freethy, Rodney Maddox, David McEvoy, Eda and John Moroney and their children, Domenica Mortati, the Profumo family: Terry, Victor, Barbara, Robert, Marty, and Edward, Paul Robinson, Myron Rottenstein, Arlene and Dan Sedgwick, Jeanne and Raymond Sierka, Rev. Douglas Verdin and Margaret Verdin.

Special thanks go to my friendly "critics" who have faithfully read each new chapter. Their suggestions were always helpful and on target with respect to the purpose of the book: Violet and Sal Auteri, Lee and David Clark, Dorothy and Walter Brand, Jeanne and James Lambert, Cleone Miller, Vivian Werner, Rev. Walter Wichmanowski.

To my brother Charles, who insisted that I write this book, I am truly indebted. He and his wife, Dorothea, have encouraged my efforts and been enthusiastic cheerleaders.

Deep gratitude is due to my brother Stephen and his wife, Clara, who have been great supporters. I can never thank Steve enough for all the time he spent meticulously combing draft after draft, offering invaluable insights and assistance.

Finally, I want to acknowledge Betty, my wife and editor. Her steadfast faith, constant encouragement, unending patience, and highly creative editorial skills helped make this book a reality. Together, we always could see the hopeful flicker of light at the end of the tunnel.

Contents

Part I.
Getting Acquainted

Memo from a Modern Methuselah:

Author's Note

THE CONCEPT FOR THIS BOOK is drawn from my experiences in a life that spans the administrations of seventeen presidents of the United States and a career of more than seventy years in the world of international business management. These years include two World Wars, the Korean War, Viet Nam, the Cold War, the Great Depression, momentous space-age scientific progress leading to moon landings and beyond, and numerous other breathtaking technological advances.

First and foremost, I am most fortunate to have been blessed with parents who, by example, imbued in each of their five children a deep reverence for God, a strict sense of duty and responsibility, and a high standard of personal ethics. For these lessons, I am forever grateful to them.

Beyond this basic early training, I have had the privilege of working with and learning from highly competent, ethical bosses who gave me many opportunities to succeed (or fail). They showed me how to prepare for the future, even by training my own successors long before there was a hint of a need for them. This opened up more opportunities for myself, because my superiors knew that the work that I would leave behind would be carried on by others who were well prepared to do my job. In turn, in fairness to my employers, I worked hard to improve my capabilities and performance within each job as if it were the last I would ever have.

In 1953 my family and associates encouraged and supported me in the risky undertaking of starting a management consulting firm. The firm grew solely on client referral to an international operation with multinational clients, backed by a highly competent dedicated staff. Looking back on those 34 rewarding years, while all of the assignments in our general practice were of importance, I truly believe that the most significant work we did involved helping our clients develop high-caliber men and women into top-drawer managers.

Essentially, I have never stopped wanting to learn throughout my life. It has not always been easy, but there have been plenty of rewarding milestones along the way. Additionally, I have had the advantage of knowing and observing, sometimes at close range, many leaders in industry, church, science, education, the military and government at home and abroad. Also, I have learned a great deal from the several generations of executives in many industries and countries to whom I have been privileged to be both mentor and friend. These all have provided truly noteworthy educational experiences.

"Retirement" for me began in Arizona at age 80. I went to ground-school to earn a student pilot's license at 84, tackled a multimedia personal computer at 86 — and am now putting the finishing touches to this book at age 88.

As a "modern Methuselah," moreover, I am eagerly looking forward to many more tomorrows as time swiftly propels me toward four score and ten. . . and a bit beyond. As the story was told often in my family, when my great-grandfather reached age 110, he remarked that the years had passed as swiftly as entering the house from the front door and going out by the back door *without stopping*. So you see, I may not be over-reaching.

It is my earnest wish that this book, as a memo from a modern Methuselah, will be of significant interest and, perhaps, of some benefit to many people in their work, family and community lives. Especially, I wish that younger men and women would find it useful in planning and working toward their own futures. This is particularly so because they will be our new leaders. Although they are and will be educated and trained for living and working with high technologies — many yet to be invented — I truly believe that the basic principles contained in this book, so essential to a fruitful, worthwhile life, never change. It always has been so and so shall it be always.

A bout this book:

How it all began

IMPROVING PERSONAL EFFECTIVENESS has its roots in the *Fotis PARFORM© System for Key Manager Resource Development.* The system evolved while serving multinational client management needs. Over a period of twenty-five years more than 200 men and women in client organizations participated in various forms of this evaluation and training program.

Early in our work in evaluating on-the-job performance of these participants it became apparent that personal effectiveness was the significant difference between those who were obviously on the "cutting edge" as gifted managers compared to those who otherwise may have had nearly identical experience and educational qualifications. This clearly became an important feature in identifying and developing individuals with high potential for steady career progress on the management track.

During the training and development phase, participants found that the focus on personal effectiveness skills was extremely productive. Over the years, positive feedback was received from many of these executives about the benefits they experienced in career and personal growth from this part of the system.

The challenge to translate what was originally a system for business management development into an individualized personal self-improvement program led to writing this practical guide to nine universally applicable people-skills.

1.	Personal Ethics	**6.**	Persuasiveness
2.	Adaptability	**7.**	Objectivity
3.	Tact	**8.**	Initiative
4.	Credibility	**9.**	Self-discipline
5.	Intercommunication		

While there may be many other individual attributes that can contribute to personal effectiveness, it has been my experience that these nine people-skills contribute most to winning confidence, respect and cooperation — whether within a family, or in a community, business or employment environment. Furthermore, these people-skills also can have an observable reciprocal effect in the positive reactions and responses of others.

Improving Personal Effectiveness is not an academic treatise on human behavior. Nor does it attempt to penetrate the cognitive aspects of the mind. Simply, it presents a selective, practical examination of these nine powerful interactive people-skills to help readers realize and reinforce their own capabilities in interpersonal encounters.

The people-skills outlined in this guide are not intended to be applied in the same way as the skills needed to outwit and overpower an opponent in a game of chess. Neither are they intended to help anyone gain an unfair advantage over others. On the contrary, the goal is to create an atmosphere where decisions and agreements can be reached in harmony so that information, directions and instructions can be given and received constructively. Most gratifying of all is to have the job done well and all parties satisfied with the outcome.

It is my firm belief that as these personal effectiveness skills become regularly grounded in a person's daily life, the effect is a more successful, mutually harmonious outcome of most interactions with others. Through ongoing self-evaluation it is possible to make the most of each new experience and continuously gain more self-assurance as we come closer to peak personal effectiveness within our own natural capabilities.

To the Reader:

How to use this book

IMPROVING PERSONAL EFFECTIVENESS is meant to be a personal ethical guide to success in winning respect, cooperation and confidence from others. This can be a vital key to leadership. And, I would add that leadership ability is essential in many aspects and dimensions of life.

To begin, the book is intentionally brief so that you will be able to skim through it easily. This will give you an over-view and lead you to more thorough reading of individual chapters in any order which seems most meaningful to you. Each chapter is written to help you find " thought-starters" for improving an individual people-skill. The elaboration on these clues comes from you, as you relate them to your own experience and situation. As you proceed, you should be able to perceive ways to apply these skills constructively to your own goals in successful interpersonal relations, whether in your family, school, work or community.

Some will find that they already have some proficiency in these people-skills, but the degree to which they practice them effectively will vary from skill to skill, individual to individual, and situation to situation. Your main effort will be to strengthen some and develop others. You made the biggest step forward when you decided to try — which shows *initiative*, one of the powerful people-skills.

Periodic review of this material, especially while the concept is new to you, may help to develop your people-skills incrementally. It is hoped that by re-reading and reconsidering the suggestions, whatever change you may desire in your interactive dealings with others will follow naturally. A successful young oil industry executive who read an advance copy of this book commented that he would like to keep it and read it about twice a year.

When you are fairly familiar with the basics of the people-skills as defined in this book, begin your Personal Effectiveness Profile©. You will find that it can be a very useful process to try to evaluate your progress in this light.

Everyone wants to succeed. But, regardless of any of the many forms that success can take, it is my perception that, if one wishes to be truly successful in life one must also be successful in dealing with others. Winning reciprocal confidence, respect and cooperation is an ethical as well as practical goal.

Part II.

Positive Personal Effectiveness

Positive Personal Effectiveness:

Winning confidence, respect and cooperation

*Only rarely and under certain
exceptional conditions is the individual
in a position to disregard relations
with other individuals.*

—SIGMUND FREUD

IT IS VIRTUALLY IMPOSSIBLE FOR ANYONE TO LIVE ALONE, totally independent of other humans. Each day in almost every activity — at home or at work, at the supermarket, on the highway — we cannot avoid interacting in some way with other people. Whether or not such interactions can be fully effective for all sides will depend largely on the manner, clarity and fairness with which we present our points of view.

Clearly, the importance of positive personal effectiveness cannot be overstated. It is natural and begins in the cradle in the interaction of child and parent. What is almost instinctive in the newborn becomes gradually more sophisticated over time. It continues to develop and is shaped throughout a life-time according to individual experiences, education, lifestyle, personality, and physical and social environments.

While we may not be fully aware of it, in nearly every per-sonal contact — whatever the purpose or subject, however important or trivial — the basic desire and underlying aim on both sides is to achieve our respective goals as amicably, eq-uitably, and often quickly, as possible. This is the premise for the dynamics of positive personal effectiveness as presented in this guide. Therefore, it seems prudent to keep it in mind as an important universal goal basic to all interpersonal encounters.

The nine powerful people-skills for *Improving Personal Effectiveness* are:

1. Personal Ethics
2. Adaptability
3. Tact
4. Credibility
5. Intercommunication
6. Persuasiveness
7. Objectivity
8. Initiative
9. Self-discipline

In general, these nine people-skills already exist within each of us in varying degrees. In many cases, we just need more individual practice and focus to strengthen them.

This is somewhat comparable to the existence of different levels of athletic competence in individuals. Outstanding athletes will acknowledge their differing levels of capability among various sports. A superbowl quarterback may be just as frustrated with his tennis or bowling as you and I, although on another level of expectations and competence. However, he knows from experience that sustained training and practice can enhance personal performance in any sport. Similarly, we need to exert continued effort and concentrated practice to improve further on the people-skills we may already possess in some degree.

Self-improvement in personal effectiveness is not an original idea. In fact, it is an old American tradition. In his *Autobiography,* one of our most successful forefathers, Benjamin Franklin described how he educated himself. Franklin's conscientious effort to increase his personal effectiveness is an interesting lesson for all of us.

Franklin admitted that early in his life he was often contentious and argumentative. Eventually he realized that although with his superior knowledge and forceful arguments he usually won the debate, he rarely gained adherents to his viewpoint. (In fact, he regretted that he even lost some friends.) This led him to see that he should be mindful always of the other person's point of view, even *when it was opposed to his,* in order to bring them both closer to their mutual objective.

His determined effort to improve what are considered here as the powerful people-skills of *intercommunication, tact* and *persuasiveness,* helped Benjamin Franklin to become enormously effective. His was a long, fruitful life, with many remarkable achievements which still influence our lives today, not the least of which was his pivotal role in the forging of the Constitution of the United States.

Although there is some overlap among the people-skills, each is treated here as an entity in itself. For example, there are similarities between *tact, intercommunication* and *persuasiveness.* However, we cannot readily substitute one for the other without diluting the meaning we wish to convey. In effect, they are like indispensable links in a stout chain. For this reason, it is extremely important to commit to developing a full understanding of the nine essential people-skills. In this way, you will be better prepared to accomplish the principal purpose of each personal encounter with greater ease and without confusion.

It is possible and desirable to continually examine, evaluate, and strengthen your own skills in order to improve your positive personal effectiveness. You might start by thinking about recent interactive experiences with others that you may have had. Try to recall your impressions at those times. Were you more comfortable in one situation than in any of the others? See if you can find a reason for that particular feeling at that time. Was it because you were able to put yourself in the other person's shoes — remembering to be tactful, for example?

Then, try to recall another interactive experience in which you felt far less comfortable about the outcome. Was it a difference in *credibility?* Was there a problem in *intercommunication?* On your part or on that of the others? Or, was there a need for more *adaptability?*

Positive personal effectiveness is achieved whenever we can ethically win confidence, respect and cooperation in our dealings with other people.

Part III.

Nine Powerful People-Skills

*P*ersonal Ethics:

The Golden Rule

*Do unto others as you would
have others do unto you.*

—THE NEW TESTAMENT

PERSONAL ETHICS FOR THE PURPOSES OF *Improving Personal Effectiveness* essentially is the practice of the Golden Rule. It is the first people-skill because it is basic to establishing and maintaining a high standard of excellence in the practice of the other powerful people-skills which are discussed in chapters to follow.

The subject of ethics has been discussed and debated over thousands of years. In the 1980's it became a hot subject at business, medical, and law schools. Hundreds of books and articles have been written on all aspects of ethics: professional, business, and many, many others. This has led to many kinds of situational ethics — as in accounting ethics, journalism ethics, medical ethics.

Why is this so? Perhaps it is because "ethics" in the abstract can be understood and appreciated, but the active practice of ethics is all too often considered somewhat unrelated to the "real world."

In current literature, concern with ethics is often likely to emphasize leg*alities* more than ethics. *"Can I get sued for doing this?"* is an entirely different question from *"Might I injure someone unjustly if I do this?"* Ethical conduct cannot be legislated; it is a self-imposed moral code by which people try to govern all of their daily actions.

Thus, *personal ethics* is an individual's commitment to the practice of positive ethical behavior as wisely expressed in the Golden Rule. The Golden Rule is an uncomplicated and universal guide; versions of it can be found in virtually every culture. When people follow it, it works well for all.

What you do not want done to yourself, do not do to others.

—CONFUCIUS

He that does what is right does it to his own advantage.

—THE KORAN

What is hateful to you do not do to your neighbor.

—THE TALMUD

But is this a practical approach to personal effectiveness? A client who became a good friend told me that his first boss told him to, "Do unto others before they do unto you." This advice created terrible tension and stress for him because he had been raised with a high standard of ethical values.

He writes, "I did continue, however, to try to learn about my job and believe in my duties and responsibilities to the company that paid my salary, to my customers, as well as to my wife and children. Eventually, I learned that most successful businessmen at the top were those that displayed a great deal of personal ethics and accepted their responsibilities to their employers, employees and shareholders." This man retired a few years ago as co-founder and president of a publicly held international high-technology business that blazed a trail in new directions for that industry.

Consistent reliance on *personal ethics* as a guiding principle in our personal encounters will often, in turn, guide or inspire others to respond on the same basis. Thus *personal ethics* can become a powerful synergistic instrument in the development and practical use of the other personal effectiveness skills — a benefit on all sides.

Good character, stemming from the practice of good ethics, is a distinctive quality of leadership. It distinguishes any leader who exhibits this characteristic from others who may simply wish to dominate or get their way without due consideration to truth, equity or fairness. By example, it inspires well-founded reciprocal confidence and trust in others.

Is there a special time or circumstance calling for personal ethics? George C. Marshall — soldier, statesman, educator — said that he lived every day as though it was being filmed in a documentary for all the world to see. This is a tough standard, but you will find that remembering it will support the other people skills and increase your effectiveness immensely.

While serving as Secretary of State, George Marshall proposed an economic assistance plan for the United States to help allies as well as former enemies in western Europe to rebuild from the ashes of World War II. One of the reasons for this was that he and President Truman could see the need to support those countries as healthy democracies in the light of the then Soviet Union's threatening power in Eastern Europe.

The historic Marshall Plan is a pragmatic example of the interactive effectiveness of the Golden Rule in international affairs. The European countries maintained their political freedom and, together with the United States, achieved unparalleled prosperity. It probably was a principal factor leading to the end of the Cold War.

Applying ethical considerations constructively in daily encounters with family, friends, business associates, or even strangers, is central to *Improving Personal Effectiveness*. It does not necessarily follow that your own wishes will always prevail in every interactive situation in which you may become involved. Whenever the views on the other side prove more appropriate than your own, the Golden Rule empowers you to react to the perceptions of others reasonably, fairly and objectively and adjust your posture sensibly in order to reach a mutually satisfactory as well as positive goal.

Personal ethics establishes in us an underlying self-assurance. Although we may not always know what tomorrow brings, we already have within ourselves the personal standard for dealing successfully with whatever may come to pass.

*A**daptability:*

Adjusting to changing circumstances

> *...changed conditions induce an almost indefinite amount of fluctuating variability, by which the whole organization is rendered in some degree plastic.*
>
> —CHARLES DARWIN

ADAPTABILITY IS OUR CAPACITY TO REACT AND ADJUST to new and changing conditions. As a people-skill, it helps us to bring into harmony our attitudes and actions in personal, family, physical, educational, religious, social, career and economic environments. Human *adaptability* makes it possible for us to adjust to these environments, often simultaneously and occasionally instantaneously.

Without *adaptability* (Darwin's plasticity) no species could have survived the rigors of the evolution of life on this planet. Human *adaptability* helped our ancestors to become incrementally stronger mentally and physically while they also developed socially — gradually gaining better control of their lives and environment.

Adaptability is still a major positive force in our continuing survival, but in a totally different context. The intellectual, educational, emotional and economic challenges of today's multidimensional environment can be just as daunting as those that over many eons forced primitive man to evolve into the creature who now approaches the next millennium. Moreover, the current pace of change seems to be at ultrasonic speed due to the steady, often disruptive, flow of revolutionary scientific, technological and sociological developments.

At the same time, at a corresponding pace, our interpersonal relations necessarily undergo continual modification. Socially, economically, politically and geopolitically, the complexity of our lives demands even more fine-tuning in how we interact with each other at school, at work, in the family, in our community — everywhere.

Relying on this inherent and positive trait of *adaptability* we can survive and grow as individuals in today's multidimensional environment. Progress in personal well-being and happiness as well as career development often depends on the degree of *adaptability* and the commonsensical way it is exercised by each of us in improving personal effectiveness.

The innate nature of human *adaptability* can be seen in the way infants adjust physically, socially and emotionally to their new world from the moment they are born. Healthy development involves continuous interactive adjustments by the child, parents and family, both consciously and involuntarily.

The child continues to learn and grow, venturing into more complex environments among ever more varying routines, and accommodates group expectations throughout life. Children's characteristic plasticity enables them to develop into unique human beings. (This is the quality that inspires all teachers.)

The required degree of *adaptability* varies with each situation. Sometimes it may be only temporary or minor. At other times it may involve coping with a life-problem so serious as to seem beyond our personal control. The necessary modification may be physical, intellectual, or even emotional. Often, it is all three.

The agent for change may be the uplifting joy at the birth of a child, the sudden jolt of the loss of a job, or grief on the death of a spouse. War, hurricanes and uncontrollable fire and floods can obliterate homes and towns, inflicting cruel tragedies and untold hardships that the resilient try to overcome. Illness might devastate a family, but *adaptability* can help it survive and be strengthened by the struggle.

Experience teaches us that however crucial or onerous the circumstances may be, *adaptability* can help us manage them better. Think of the countless individuals who refuse to be handicapped by their disabilities and develop highly creative ways of transforming daunting difficulties into inspiring successes. Helen Keller, without sight or hearing, learned to communicate with resounding effectiveness and to illuminate the world with her brilliant and inspiring concepts. Paraplegics in wheelchairs play basketball.

In such seemingly impossible triumphs of the human spirit, thanks to the gift of human *adaptability,* each of us can find inspiration and renewed confidence in ourselves and in our capacity to overcome and become even better.

Adaptability is a valuable people-skill for improving personal effectiveness as we interface with others. In these interactions, inevitably, we will find it necessary in some way to adapt as much as we can to each others' needs, expectations, strengths, weaknesses, tolerances and emotions. In doing so we reinforce the positive aspect of our continuing growth as human beings. Patience and good judgment in making timely appropriate adjustments in attitude or behavior can prevent trying situations from becoming unmanageable.

Virtually every career path demands some degree of *adaptability.* The world itself, in a continual ferment, is being constantly restructured socially, technologically, economically, politically and even ecologically. Entire industries, governments, professions, military and educational systems are being reorganized every day because of competition, attrition, mergers, inventions, elections, new laws and regulations, as well as mandated environmental priorities.

On a personal level, the impact on those affected by such global dynamics poses numerous burdensome corollary problems for themselves and their families — be they students, corporate executives, entry-level workers, religious leaders, military personnel, self-employed, unemployed or retired.

Knowing that change is inevitable and far-reaching, we can try to accept this as an inescapable feature of life in the Twenty-First Century and prepare to deal with it confidently in positive ways. As old jobs are lost, more new jobs — often requiring new skills — are being created. Predictably, those who are willing to accept retraining or relocation can survive with excellent prospects to prosper.

Sometimes the necessary adjustment can be painfully radical, even traumatic. In a downsizing layoff, for instance, affected workers may find themselves catapulted into different work worlds: a jet pilot takes a job as a teacher; a mining superintendent turns to selling real estate, and on and on. Somehow they all manage to adapt and in most cases go on to new accomplishments as the economic climate inevitably completes another cycle.

Each successful transition in life and career broadens our scope, enhances our tolerance for change and reinforces our *adaptability*. The interactive effect strengthens our self-reliance, sharpens our capabilities, and increases the confidence others have in us. A capable senior manager will recognize, appreciate, rely on and eventually reward subordinates who can change gears sensibly, smoothly and, therefore, successfully.

A manager may play many roles on any given day — the wise counselor, the stern disciplinarian, the compassionate consoler, the inspiring teacher, the group spokesman and defender, the messenger from higher headquarters. It takes *adaptability* as well as all the other interactive people-skills to effectively assume these roles at any time and even at the same time, depending on the circumstances.

It is important to be mindful of the degree of *adaptability* that may be comfortable for others. Spouse, children, parents, boss, coworkers and associates — they all have different tolerances for change. It is imperative that we maintain an awareness of their personal levels of tolerance when we are considering changes that will affect them. By making allowances for these differences in a practical way we can hope to preclude or defuse resistance and needless confrontations.

Adaptability does not imply indiscriminate change. It is only when changes are desirable, necessary or inevitable that *adaptability* can be beneficial. Not only is it folly to change anything simply for the sake of change, but it is crucial to avoid making the cardinal error of effecting the right changes at the wrong time or for the wrong reasons.

New opportunities abound for the forward-thinking individual who anticipates possible new directions and is willing to adapt to the inevitability of change realistically. The "utility man" on a baseball team gets a contract because he has translated his adaptability into versatility. *Learning to learn can be an important key to a fruitful life.*

Adaptability reinforces all the other essential people-skills. Here again we recognize that each is a link vital in the personal effectiveness chain of *personal ethics, adaptability, tact, credibility, intercommunication, persuasiveness, objectivity, initiative,* and *self-discipline.*

*T*act:

Sensitivity to others' perceptions

The nearer you come into relation with a person, the more necessary do tact and courtesy become.

—OLIVER WENDELL HOLMES

TACT IS A WAY OF DEALING WITH OTHERS thoughtfully and with genuine concern for their feelings. Sensitivity to what is appropriate in a given situation together with the ability to speak, lead or act without offending are the hallmarks of *tact*. *Tact* can be regarded as the "great facilitator" in all mutually successful interpersonal encounters. It does not work alone, but strengthens the value of the other people-skills.

A lifetime of working with many people on many levels has proven to me that this essential people-skill is all too often neglected in the rush of business as usual. For instance, competent individuals possessing intelligence as well as many of the other people-skills outlined in this guide may still falter because they have not yet recognized the importance of *tact* in smooth interpersonal relations.

We begin to learn *tact* from our parents. Good manners and courtesy are basic expressions of this people-skill.

Tact cannot be contrived; it should be neither obsequious in behavior, nor condescending in attitude. Rooted in ethics and the Golden Rule, *tact*, ideally, should be accorded to everyone — not to just a selected few, but to *everyone* — in the same manner as we would like them to treat ourselves.

Practiced according to the Golden Rule, *tact* becomes effortless and natural in a truly effective leader. This reminds me of one of the most tactful people I have ever known. He was my copy chief on my first job in advertising. His was an outstanding professional reputation for leadership in the industry.

On my first day on the job, many years ago, I tentatively brought my initial effort to him for review. He looked it over deliberately, his hand holding a blue pencil hovering over each line of my copy, while I waited apprehensively for what seemed an eternity. At last he looked up and said, "This is just fine — but would you mind if I suggest that you find a word that is a little more compatible with your theme than this one?" Drawing a blue circle around the offending word, he added in a kindly voice, "I'm sure you can." I not only found the right word, but in the process I significantly sharpened the theme — which I realized eventually was exactly what he expected to happen!

This was a lesson I never forgot. He was not only brilliant and creative, but as an effective manager he considered the feelings of the lowliest, greenest subordinate, and treated him with genuine concern and regard. He was never too busy to be tactful.

Lacking *tact* can be a costly impediment to personal effectiveness. We all know someone who takes pride in "telling it like it is." Often these people will complain that being "too honest" denied them a promotion or resulted in the loss of a job or a friend. If the truth were known, we might find *tact* as the missing element in their ability to interface harmoniously with family, associates and friends.

Such people mistakenly equate "telling it like it is" with being honest. They are often puzzled or feel slighted when others react negatively to a sort of overkill in forthrightness. Quite obviously one can never be "too honest," but sometimes one might drift into the disagreeable habit of being tactlessly and painfully frank.

How can we avoid unnecessary conflict with someone who is taking a totally arbitrary posture of disagreement? Compare the statement, *"Please tell me a little more about how you came to this conclusion,"* with, *"I don't agree with you."* The first approach might prevent reactive antagonism; the second is more likely to cause it. Even when it still is necessary to proceed without total agreement, by having exhibited respect for another person's opinions we may at least have set the stage for a more positive future interaction with that person.

As a practical guide to improving *tact,* we would like to consider three basic dimensions: perception, discretion and empathy.

Perception is defined here as the ability to continually and quickly interpret for yourself the more subtle aspects other peoples' statements, actions, reactions or non-actions during interpersonal encounters. Working on our perceptive ability means building a better awareness of other peoples' sensitivities.

There are times when we can avoid a suddenly arisen mutually embarrassing situation by tactfully concluding an interview or conversation that we perceive is becoming uncomfortable. We may not always know why or what happened, but with practice we can learn to sense beyond the obvious and so ease what otherwise might become a potentially untenable situation.

Our perception can be enhanced by the continual practice of reviewing significant interactions in a day, asking ourselves questions like, *"Did I grasp fully the significance of X's remarks in that situation?...What was he really trying to tell me?...Could I have anticipated such a surprisingly vehement reaction to my suggestions?"*

Discretion is the art of "cautious reservation." When we listen carefully to what is being said, not reacting impulsively, we can create an atmosphere within which views can be exchanged open-mindedly and the possibility of unpleasant confrontations minimized. Discretion on both sides enables each party to handle thorny matters more prudently, thus enhancing the chances of more productive ongoing relationships.

Discretion also implies respect for confidential information and for keeping it that way. This helps to build *credibility*, another essential people-skill.

Self-control under pressure is a powerful aspect of discretion. It involves recognizing what not to do or say — and when to do or say nothing — in critical situations. Most of us have experienced the consequences when someone (often ourselves) failed to assess beforehand the extent to which a word spoken, a decision made, or an action taken would impact on others.

Empathy lies in our capacity for relating to another person's underlying feelings, concerns and attitudes — an effort to put ourselves in the other person's shoes. With it, we are less apt to press "hot buttons" inadvertently. Because empathetic people are appreciative of the views of others, they can more likely present their own positions tactfully.

Empathy is not sympathy. We might empathize and therefore understand why a person failed to meet a commitment or obligation, but still not condone the result. For example, a supervisor might see that heavy rush-hour traffic presents a problem to a chronically tardy subordinate, but would not accept it as a valid excuse for repeated lateness. Tactfully, the supervisor could suggest that this subordinate find another route or start earlier in order to be on time and, just as importantly, avoid developing a reputation for unreliability.

Although perception, discretion and empathy have been discussed here separately, they are inseparable interactive elements of *tact*. Whether we find it necessary to correct a wrong impression, critique the job someone has done, lead others in a team effort, listen to an ancient joke, or discuss a child's failing grade in geometry with his or her math teacher, the manner in which we do it has more chance of being effective if it is tactful and appropriate to the situation.

There is another dimension to our reflections on *tact* relative to our growing national concern about hostility, anger and violence in behavior and words. *Tact* can be a powerful remedial tool for each of us to use to promote civility, at least within our own orbits. It is, after all, nothing more or less than a function of our mutual respect for each other as individuals with our own opinions, convictions and sensitivities. Treating our neighbors with consideration can motivate them to treat us and others in the same way.

Tact speaks eloquently for *personal ethics* and the Golden Rule.

C redibility:

Earning trust
and confidence

Wherever a man goes...
his character goes with him.

—AFRICAN PROVERB

Credibility is an essential attribute that is built on the elements of integrity, reliability, veracity, competence and commitment. *Credibility* shines in those persons who are ethically motivated. In fact, it joins *personal ethics* as a catalyst in the successful application of the other people-skills essential to *Improving Personal Effectiveness*. Together, they energize the development of these skills. *Credibility* lends its power to personal effectiveness in that it earns the genuine respect, trust and confidence of others.

Without *credibility,* trust and confidence among people would be seriously impaired. Interpersonal relations would regress to *caveat emptor* — let the buyer beware. Family relationships could suffer terribly. Neighbors would become wary of neighbors. International trade would suffer to the point of becoming chaotic. Governments would fall. Obviously, this is not likely to ever happen universally at the same time. But the thought of the possibility, though "far fetched," is a sobering reminder of the global importance of *credibility* in our words and actions.

We can better understand how to build *credibility* by considering five basic elements: integrity, reliability, veracity, competence, and commitment.

Integrity: People who have integrity firmly uphold an integrated, coherent, cohesive set of moral values. They exhibit an astute sense of *personal ethics* and probity in all their dealings. They are trusted by others because of their consistent practice of the Golden Rule.

When unusual or special circumstances prevent a full explanation of a situation, we may have to rely "on faith" for acceptance by others of our actions or a sudden decision. In such cases, we need not fear the possibility of disapproval if we already have a record of integrity that establishes confidence in our *credibility.*

In the wholesale diamond industry a contract is often made with a handshake in transactions involving millions of dollars. There is trust that the merchandise will be delivered and paid for as agreed. This works because all of the members of that industry are conscious of the daily importance of maintaining the integrity of their reputations.

Reliability: To be credible is to be predictably reliable. As an element of *credibility*, reliability automatically assures others that all obligations made will be fulfilled. Evidence of reliability lies in the consistency with which we deliver on commitments, promises and statements.

Our *credibility* may also be dependent at times upon the reliability of others. At home or at work, do you depend on an assistant, a vendor, or some outside service to carry out a task efficiently and within agreed-upon time parameters? If, for instance, snags develop in the fulfillment of any of these services that cannot be remedied in a timely fashion, your reliability and, therefore, your own *credibility* may be at stake! Responsibility to our families, customers, bosses, or patients indicates that we be fully aware and confidently assured of the level of reliability in those on whom our word may depend.

Veracity: A habitual desire for truth and accuracy builds unquestionable personal *credibility*. In a job situation, for instance, your word as to the cost and fulfillment of agreements — or assessment of the value of a proposal — would be respected because of your reputation and track record. An opinion, recommendation, or report from a person with a reputation for veracity would be given credence without delay or question.

Truthfulness is closely linked to knowledge and training. There are people who never can say, "I don't know." They will try to extemporize instead of offering to find the information required. Have you ever been sent down the wrong road by faulty directions from a stranger whom you asked for assistance? Imagine how this person would feel if his doctor "winged it" when writing a prescription!

Competence: The ability to apply one's knowledge, experience and conscientious effort to the optimal solution of a given problem promotes personal *credibility*. An untrained but dependable individual can build competence through study, experience and hard work.

For instance, an inexperienced CPA, no matter how honest and reliable, is not ready to be a credible candidate for the Federal Reserve Board. (On the other hand, a Rhodes scholarship in economics would not automatically make an individual with a reputation for being a "slick operator" any more credible a candidate for the position.) Competence and confidence are earned through demonstrated dependable performance.

A competent person will not become distracted or easily panicked when, for instance, circumstances begin to show that a deadline may not be met. This person is capable of quickly moving to identify the problem and then find ways to enlist cooperation to correct the situation, even when the cause may lie within someone else's area of responsibility. *Instead of stopping to affix blame, a competent individual will try to find a timely solution to the problem and secure the co-operation of others in implementing it.*

Commitment: When we undertake a project, we want to commit all our expertise, talents and energy to see that it is properly completed. By our example we are then able to engage the firm commitment of others to the enterprise. This is another indication of the interactive aspect in personal effectiveness.

Commitments and promises are of necessity constantly being made in anyone's life and they cover an extremely wide range. Some of them are self-liquidating, *e.g.,* school enrollment; others go on for many years, *e.g.,* employment; and a few might last a lifetime, *e.g.,* marriage. Other people will trust in the *credibility* of an individual by the depth and sincerity perceived in his or her commitment — whether in a family, team, church, business or any other group or organization. As always, a leader's past performance creates a track record which builds up *credibility.*

Without much effort, we all can think of someone who exemplifies *credibility* to us; someone who never betrayed our trust and influenced our lives. I think first of my own father. And then, I think of the "Father of our Country," George Washington. Here was a very credible human being whose leadership was solicited and affirmed throughout his life. The "cherry tree" myth illustrates the legendary quality of his reputation for honesty. Commanding the forces of the colonies in the Revolution, he was able to keep the colonies united in their goals. Later, as the first President of the United States, he set precedents and standards which have endured for over 200 years. Sheer force of character made George Washington a giant in our national history.

Intercommunication:

Dynamic expression

*When I am getting ready to reason
with a man, I spend one-third of my
time thinking about myself and what I
am going to say – and two-thirds
thinking about him and what
he is going to say.*

—ABRAHAM LINCOLN

INTERCOMMUNICATION IS THE SYNTHESIZER, coordinating
all of the other people-skills — *personal ethics, adaptability,
tact, credibility, persuasiveness, objectivity, initiative* and *self-
discipline*. Each of these skills has its own positive value in
interpersonal relations. *Intercommunication* capability creates
the power to use all of them most effectively.

Intercommunication as presented in this chapter empha-
sizes the multidimensional aspects of communication as a
personal effectiveness skill. This was recognized by Abraham
Lincoln, who paid twice as much attention to the concerns the
other person might have in mind in relation to the purpose of
their contemplated meeting as he devoted to what he himself
was going to say.

In this quotation, Lincoln also shows us his appreciation of
the complexity of communication and the importance of relevant planning and preparation beforehand. Clearly, he was
looking ahead, trying to envision a mutually satisfactory end
result even before the meeting took place.

When we think of Lincoln as a basically self-taught country
boy who became a very sophisticated lawyer, debater and
politician, we are compelled to appreciate his self-developed
skill as a positive communicator. What better example could
we have than the President of the United States who successfully led our country through its worst national crisis?

In personal *intercommunication,* we aim for a response in
some form or other. We naturally seek to engender positive
interactions with any or all with whom we are dealing at all
times. A good communicator conveys a message, ideas, information and intentions, clearly and concisely, while — as a
reciprocal interaction — listening, hearing, and evaluating the
comments, interests and feelings on the other side. Whether
dealing with child, spouse, neighbor or boss, our goal is to
understand them and to have them understand us as well.

Positive *intercommunication* involves *listening*. This cannot be overemphasized: listen carefully, intently, and sincerely to what other people have to say so that you really hear their message. This is the only way to get meaningful feedback on their feelings and expectations. Listen attentively to their concerns. Even if you doubt the validity of their thinking, you will better understand how to deal with them. Remember, always *listen... listen... listen!*

Another point to be remembered: what is unsaid is often as meaningful as what is said. This is especially important, whether communicating orally, or in writing. Silence can be resounding. At times, saying nothing can say it all!

In addition to noting what is being said, we want to be aware of nonverbal signs, or body language. Impatience, for instance, may be expressed in a shifting of bodily position. Also, keep in mind, this is true for ourselves as well as the individuals with whom we may be speaking. When you feel your arms folding across your chest — or see this in another person — you can sense a mind that is closing or resisting the message. Try to find a mutually acceptable solution as soon as possible, even if it means tactfully leaving sooner than you planned.

The effectiveness of your message will always be reflected in the response you get back — whether in action, attitude, or words. These responses offer an excellent ongoing opportunity for evaluating yourself as a communicator. For the purposes of this book, there are four fundamental areas of *intercommunication*.

Intercommunication One-On-One: The great advantage to one-on-one oral *intercommunication* is that it is possible for each side to personally project an idea or a request and get timely feedback as to its acceptability. An inflection or a tone of voice can make a huge difference in a message. In this way, each participant has the opportunity before the conversation is over to take immediate positive clarifying or corrective action.

It is helpful to listen "actively." Sometimes we can verify our understanding by simply repeating or rephrasing what the other person has said. In turn, this also encourages a conscientious effort by others to listen just as attentively.

There are times when a telephone call may be an unwelcome intrusion. (Timing is always a factor in personal effectiveness.) A simple, "Is this a good time for you?" can make a big difference in how your message is received. This tactful question can be a constructive, positive improvement over "How are you?" as a conversation opener. A business call may find your client on his way out to an important meeting; a social call may find people at dinner. In each case, if you just plunge right in you may not get the attention you need. However, if you do make sure that your client or friend is free to talk with you, your call will be more effective.

When a conversation is initiated by someone else, our interest should remain the same. We want to know where this person is "coming from;" we want to fully understand his or her point of view. It is neither fair, tactful, nor even good judgment, for one to jump to a conclusion or frame a reply while supposedly listening attentively.

Written Intercommunication: The written word can be more consequential than the spoken word, wherever it may fall on the information highway — from an ordinary letter to E-Mail. In written communications we do not have the advantage of the nuances of the spoken word. On the other hand, written communication provides a record that is subject to thoughtful evaluation before either side takes whatever action the situation may dictate.

Clear, thoughtful understanding of the concept we are trying to communicate, consideration of the receiver of the report, letter or memorandum, and fluency in writing are essential. This comes with practice and skill in the use of the appropriate medium. There are many sources of refresher and advanced instruction in this important skill in community colleges and adult education programs. Reading material in your field and in general is a good writing skill-builder.

Intercommunication Within a Small Group: The ability to contribute constructively to group thought, deliberation, agreement and action would normally develop from family experiences. Unfortunately, as families get smaller and the members busier, this ability can remain under-developed. It is a skill that is extremely valuable in situations where a consensus on which to base policy or other decisions is essential. This ability is equally useful within family, club, jury, faculty, committee or departmental meetings.

Perhaps you can recall a recent meeting of four or five people. Do you remember the dynamics of that small group's interaction? For instance, who had the facts? Were you prepared for certain attitudes and reactions? Were some members too dogmatic, or, on the other hand, perhaps too superficial in their attitudes? Who were those whose contributions were "on target" with respect to the topic under discussion? Whose opinions prevailed? Was the meeting a success or was it a waste of valuable time as far as its purpose was concerned?

If we make it a habit to evaluate small group *intercommunication* experiences, the answers to such questions can be valuable self-taught lessons for developing powerful insights. Before very long, one would be able to sense these dynamics — before, after, and while in a small group situation — and effectively influence the results in relation to group assignments and goals.

Speaking to an Audience: It can be more difficult for some of us to communicate formally, or even informally, to a listening group or audience. Many people have not had, or have avoided, experience in this area. Have you ever found yourself at a large meeting, with a good suggestion to offer, but uncomfortable about taking the microphone? When you have confidence in the content of your message and are prepared for the attitude the audience may reflect in its mood and its expectations, you may find that it is not as difficult as you feared.

The ability to speak effectively in public can be an invaluable tool, useful in community, church, school, and professional activities. There is no telling when, where or for whom the occasion may arise. The opportunity may come for a pediatrician to address a convention, or an individual to be a lay leader of a church, or a student to run for class office, or a taxpayer to become involved in community planning. A

CEO in the oil industry recently told me that investing in a public speaking course — to which he had to rush after a grueling day's work — helped him to go from the oilfield to a management position at the headquarters of his firm.

Now may be your time to start working on it. It can be self-developed by practice. Or, you might look into the public speaking seminars and courses available in your community. Just remember, Winston Churchill — one of the greatest orators and communicators of the 20th Century — suffered from a stammer and a lisp that he was able to overcome…

Persuasiveness:

Convincing
with credibility

*You can preach a better sermon with
your life than with your lips.*

— OLIVER GOLDSMITH

PERSUASIVENESS IS THE ABILITY TO GAIN APPROVAL, acceptance or agreement when presenting our ideas, plans,
opinions, or suggestions to others. *Persuasiveness* is a valuable
human attribute, a skill found in almost every outstanding
leader. Used with integrity, it can gain mutual cooperation and
satisfaction and therefore greater success in our dealings with
other people.

As a positive people-skill, *persuasiveness* works well for
both sides only when the purpose in trying to convince others
is well founded. Otherwise, such efforts may cause problems
that generate skepticism about an individual's *credibility*, and

gradually erode that individual's reputation. When this happens, to paraphrase another of Abraham Lincoln's remarks, any efforts to persuade would be no more successful than trying to penetrate the hard shell of a turtle with a straw. In fact, the dark side of *persuasiveness* lies in those who would use this people-skill for selfish, even potentially harmful, purposes.

Persuasiveness as discussed in *Improving Personal Effectiveness* derives its power from the people-skills of *credibility*, *intercommunication* and *tact*. In effect, it is more than the sum of its parts.

It is not necessary to change our personalities to become more persuasive. People can learn to be more persuasive and remain uniquely themselves. To test this idea, choose any three presidents of the United States and, no matter whom you choose, you would undoubtedly recognize three quite dissimilar personalities and temperaments. For instance, Abraham Lincoln is remembered generally as being homespun; Woodrow Wilson as academic; and Calvin Coolidge as laconic. Yet, each was professionally highly successful and politically persuasive enough to become nominated and elected to the highest office of our land! If you were to continue this exercise in the same vein, you would find similar variances in individuality among all the presidents since George Washington. Each had his own distinctive persona. Yet, each attained the same high political goal. This clearly tells us, whatever our aims may be, it is best to be ourselves.

The balance of this chapter is devoted to the subtle interplay of *credibility, intercommunication* and *tact* within the overall people-skill of *persuasiveness*. You may also find it useful to go back and review the previous chapters dealing with each of these skills individually.

Credibility: *Persuasiveness* often forms an integral or inseparable part of a person's well-deserved reputation for *credibility*. It is derived from competence, conviction, and dedication to ethically-driven behavior. For instance, we tend to trust a highly credible doctor's diagnosis and treatment recommendation implicitly.

As a people-skill, *persuasiveness* does not necessarily require the eloquence of an orator nor the exhortation of a crusader. As a practical matter, any form of exaggeration could be seriously counterproductive to our efforts to improve personal effectiveness. A fluent command of words or even supercreative ideas can have no validity if there is no substantive support for the credibility of what is said or done.

Let's say you are presenting a recommendation to your superiors for a significant new direction for your organization. It will help you to be persuasive if you submit a proposal containing all of the relevant facts. You would assemble reliable estimates of costs, markets, competition, regulatory or legal implications, time considerations and other important factors, before proceeding to offer a valid assessment of the chances of success. You also would present the advantages and disadvantages of each existing alternative to the proposed new direction so that you can show decisively the validity of the recommended course of action.

The relevant data and aspects may vary with differing organizational situations; but the indispensability of backup credible data and information still remains the cornerstone for viable presentations or proposals. In some instances you may not be immediately required to present supporting data. Nevertheless, be sure to have it ready at hand should the need to use it arise. The confidence that comes from having "done your homework" enhances your *persuasiveness*.

Your sincere belief in the benefit to others of your theories or opinions makes you better able to present them in a credible, clear-cut manner so your purpose can be easily understood. A very successful executive told me that many years ago, while still in college, he was sure of one thing — he did not want to be a salesman. Yet, soon after graduating, in order to make a living, he found himself in a part-time position trying to sell electric refrigerators door-to-door to families who were still using iceboxes.

Seeing firsthand so many desirable advantages to potential users in having this new appliance — convenience, sanitation, health benefits, and cost savings in terms of time gained and wasteful food spoilage avoided — eventually, he said, he grew to feel almost like a "refrigerator missionary." As he rang doorbells up and down the hallways of huge apartment buildings in New York City, to his own growing amazement, he sold quite a few refrigerators. He practiced faithfully this worthwhile lesson of the persuasive power of truth and value to the customer throughout a highly rewarding career as a successful corporate marketing executive.

Intercommunication: This important aspect of *persuasiveness* has been outlined at length in Chapter 6. Now here are a few thought-starters that may help you to more effectively present your ideas and gain serious consideration, if not always complete acceptance:

❖ Clearly indicate your purpose.

❖ Hold interest by being brief, succinct.

❖ Say it in a friendly, self-assured tone.

❖ Accomplish more with better ideas and fewer words.

❖ Pinpoint clearly, concisely.

❖ Eliminate "redundum."

❖ Forego glibness.

❖ Be transitional; don't jump around.

❖ Keep an eye on the positive.

❖ Be sure your cause is fair and legitimate.

Tact: There seems to be no doubt that many highly persuasive individuals appear to be drawn naturally to other people. On the surface, it does seem to be effortless for them to make new friends and supporters. However, as we witness their successes, we can recognize their adherence to certain basic elements of *tact* — perception, discretion and empathy — at work in their interpersonal actions. As a matter of fact, without these elements, their *persuasiveness* could be superficial and short lived.

Those who are more persuasive usually make an effort to understand the attitudes of their friends, family and associates. They are likely to have the sensitivity to anticipate what others might want or might need to hear and can perceive how far to elicit and pursue thoughts and ideas with them. Such individuals can empathize and therefore establish rapport easily by being considerate, listening actively, and identifying mutual interests, problems and goals.

Seemingly, there is no limit to where *persuasiveness* can constructively help us to reach a desired end result without undue argument or delay. We can gain more than agreement and cooperation; we can establish mutually more productive, amicable, and longer-lasting interpersonal relations.

Objectivity:

An unbiased perspective

*Before tackling any specific
question we first ought to ponder
at length and impartially those
truths which have presented
themselves to us.*

—RENE DESCARTES

OBJECTIVITY IS THE ABILITY TO EVALUATE the relevant
elements of a situation uninfluenced by emotion, belief, con-
jecture or personal preference. Observing *objectivity*,
maintaining an unbiased perspective when dealing with others, and doing so fairly and even handedly, is vital to
achieving positive personal effectiveness. Avoiding hasty judg-
ments or anything that suggests the arbitrary imposition of
one's will or opinion fosters trust and respect for our decisions. *Objectivity* is linked closely to *credibility*.

Conscious exercise of *objectivity* forces us to accept the basic truths of an issue as we find them, whether we may be pleased or displeased, like or dislike our findings. The goal is to be fair, impartial and substantive in our conclusions. *Objectivity* is the filter that clarifies the air. At the heart of *objectivity* is the premise that applicable truths must prevail in all our conclusions, even when the results might be inconvenient to us.

Once we adopt an unbiased perspective, the practical and positive effects of *objectivity* as a people-skill are wide-ranging.

Open-mindedness is indispensable to *objectivity*. Open-mindedness implies being receptive to new ideas, learning new skills, and generally keeping abreast of what is happening in the main spheres of interests in life — family, professional, community, religious, educational, political, scientific. Sooner or later, most of us are going to be computer literate — just as most of us eventually embraced air travel instead of railroads or ships as the most economic way to travel in terms of time and costs. Open-mindedness is a sterling attribute and it is wise to keep it alive in our consciousness at all times and throughout a lifetime.

Open-mindedness in life allows us the freedom of possible alternative choices. A closed mind robs us of this clear advantage.

In a climate of objectivity there can be reciprocally affirmative results. We inspire confidence in others to express or pursue their new ideas with us and to discuss openly unusual problems or critical issues, personally or within a group. In such an unthreatening atmosphere differences or concerns can be considered rationally and, therefore, discussed amiably and constructively, usually with more positive results.

One receptive mind opens up another. A spouse wishes to change careers; an assistant is eager to experiment in new directions; a student is anxious about college scholarships — what will encourage them to seek our counsel? They need to know from experience that we will listen open-mindedly and think objectively with them. The interactive results of such exchanges can be creative, beneficial and far-reaching for all sides.

Freeing us from prejudice, *objectivity* enables us to judge a person fairly by character, capability and conduct. This helps us to offer as unbiased an evaluation or opinion as possible. Whether giving or receiving criticism, we wish to be fair and objective about it. Instead of overlooking areas where improvement may be called for, either side might approach them objectively and tactfully so that critical observation can be of mutual benefit. This is another basic, interactive aspect of *objectivity* as a people-skill.

Objective teamwork can help to focus a team's resources. Have you ever been on a team or committee with too many self-styled superstars? Were the results successful? The reason for any team's existence is attainment of the group's goal through pooling the various individual skills and talents of the members. *Objectivity* helps the leader and each team member to concentrate on the team goals without letting personal feelings interfere. Time can be saved and obstructive friction minimized or totally avoided when every member of a group remembers this.

Whether on the job, on a committee, or in a community or sports environment, team members usually are chosen individually because of their special competence. Once the goal and program or game-plan are agreed on, it is extremely important that team members individually and collectively maintain the highest degree of *objectivity*. Each can then make his or her best possible contribution to the common goal.

Personal biases about the talents of the other members, the game-plan, or the ultimate value of the project, can only distract from the business at hand and lead to counterproductive ends. In any group enterprise, the most direct approach toward overall effectiveness is the individual's objective approach.

Predicaments that force difficult choices require *objectivity* not only to make the decisions, but to feel personally comfortable with them. The ability to make such choices with confidence is based on knowledge, experience and habitual objective assessment of issues. A physician may have to make a crucial decision about treatment for a patient. A lawyer may have to advise a client on a choice of pleas. A parent may have to set limits on a child's extracurricular activities. Each has an obligation to be objective.

Similarly, we too can learn to continually examine and responsibly evaluate for ourselves many aspects of our career, home, social, intellectual, political, and financial environments. Training ourselves not to allow prejudice or bias to influence our decisions and actions can produce beneficial results and improve our personal effectiveness.

Personal career status should be subjected to our ongoing objective evaluation. Better than waiting "until something better comes along" is maintaining a self-awareness of where you are, how well you are doing, and where opportunities might develop. Some individuals can easily fall into thinking they are indispensable. I well remember a high-level engineering executive who expected to become president of his company. He was so sure the company could never do without him that he ignored warnings about his habitual inconsiderate way of dealing with others. Ultimately, he was forced to accept a "golden parachute" and retire at age-52. This illustrates sadly how he lost his perceived indispensability when he lost his *objectivity* in self-appraisal. As a result, he, his family, and his employers were all casualties.

Reviewing our persistent attitudes, beliefs, or routines will forestall their tendency to solidify into deeply ingrained intellectual habits. Such habits, if not periodically re-examined, can stagnate and harden into the shape of unjustified prejudice with unsuspected rigidity. An inflexible disposition limits our ability to grasp the fact that some new ideas have significantly replaced older concepts. In effect, this forfeits our opportunity to interact effectively with others who have recognized and accepted these new ideas. It can even engender indifference, avoidance, resentment and antipathy in ourselves, among groups and with other individuals. For instance, in the negative implications of the so-called "generation gap" lies a kind of intransigence on both sides of the gap. Objective self-analysis and evaluation of new cultural, social, or economic phenomena can help ease this problem.

Fairness is another desired outcome of *objectivity*. The reality of this is profoundly felt in the area of performance evaluation. Job evaluations or classroom grades, for instance, tend to be arrived at and accepted more objectively when they are based on predetermined and pre-understood performance standards. An individual who has achieved or exceeded the specified performance requirements deserves to receive the established rating, award, or compensation, regardless of the personal feelings of the evaluator. On the same basis, where a performance falls below standards, *objectivity* on both sides dictates that appropriate recommendations be given and taken without prejudice. Fairness — essential in a supervisor, parent or teacher — will prevail where *objectivity* rules.

One final note: As you explore *Improving Personal Effectiveness*, it is important to develop the habit of evaluating yourself, especially at the outset. For instance, it is recommended that you try to recall and assess some of your interactive experiences — reflecting on where you hit a home run and where it was only a two-bagger; and on how you could have done better. For those who may be inclined to be either too lenient or too harsh when evaluating themselves, *objectivity* can rescue the self-evaluation process. *Objectivity* becomes even more meaningful when you work on your Personal Effectiveness Profile© in Part Five.

Initiative:

Getting a headstart

There are twenty ways of going to a point...
but set out at once on one.

— RALPH WALDO EMERSON

INITIATIVE IS THE SELF-MOTIVATION to translate opportunities and ideas into *realistic* action. It is a significant people-skill in a leader or a pioneer in any field, and it is essential for true success in every career or enterprise.

Initiative triggers within an individual the need to act on original ideas, to address important matters that should or must be confronted, and to rise to opportunities that are waiting to be capitalized. The continuing growth and economic strength of the United States of America, or any nation, is based on the daily renewal of the *initiative* of citizens at all levels of its society who recognize opportunity and move in to meet its challenge.

When something of consequence needs to be done without undue delay, we have to rely on *initiative*. In urgent situations where there is no one else on hand who is capable and willing to take on this responsibility, the person who acts on his or her own *initiative* often can produce impressive results — results that otherwise might never have been achievable had the opportunity for timely action been lost. As an illustration, David Sarnoff's life and the history of communication were profoundly changed on April 14, 1912, with the first faint wireless telegraph message about the sinking of the Titanic. For seventy-two hours he stayed at his wireless telegraph key in New York City, becoming a conduit of this wrenching story to the rest of the country. *Initiative* at that moment in time gained recognition for Sarnoff, as well as momentum for the development of this early form of radio. This personal effectiveness skill was always a factor David Sarnoff's long career as a pioneer and a principal in the history of radio and television.

In critical situations where time constraints dictate speedy action we must be ready to recognize and assess quickly the positive and negative factors involved. Anticipating possible contingencies keeps one alert. Conscious practice in objectively evaluating alternate or hypothetical possibilities in likely situations is another key to developing *initiative*. Very often, we must make a decision and do the best we can *now!* Success in stealing second base on a split-second *initiative* comes with prior mental and physical preparation, along with competence and a desire for excellence.

By using our best judgment, quickly weighing the consequences of action versus inaction, we are able to choose what seems to be the wisest course to follow — without hesitation! Many may tend to fear ridicule by others or be disinclined to risk failure. Christopher Columbus and other great explorers, on many frontiers, got out in front when failure might have cost them their reputations if not their lives. After having weighed and found the odds favorable for success, those who are ready and capable to take the *initiative* are apt to find themselves on the cutting-edge personally or as group leaders.

When we initiate action, there are times when we need the support of others in implementing our decision if it is to succeed. The desirability of maintaining an awareness of the effect our actions may have on others as an important ingredient in making prudent decisions, mentioned often in *Improving Personal Effectiveness*, is emphasized here. Whatever risks we may incur in taking the *initiative*, the results should be beneficial to everyone concerned. This is one way to earn cooperation and *credibility*.

While taking the *initiative* usually involves making a firm decision for immediate action, it need not necessarily be dramatic, heroic, or even dynamic. It can be as simple as deciding to write a letter or make a telephone call that may, for the moment, seem important only to you and perhaps someone else.

Opportunities to exercise *initiative* arise many times in any day: Do you perceive a need to develop a solution — a fat-free recipe, a tool for an arthritic hand? Do you perceive a need to say something helpful or hopeful? Do you perceive a need to present a new point of view? Do you perceive a need to mediate a disagreement? In any case, try to see what, if anything, you can do about it...and do it!

Five key elements of *initiative* are anticipation, good judgment, energy, action and follow-through.

Anticipation is the habit of thinking and planning ahead. It is the first element in building our *initiative* capabilities. By always sharpening our perspective on the future — personal, professional, local, national, international — we can prepare ourselves for parenthood, competition, technical advances, desirable career opportunities and changes, or retirement. A fine-tuned antenna can pay off with a great headstart some day.

We can see the practical value of anticipation all around us. As an example, many people might dismiss the idea of buying a house as being too farfetched in view of their current financial circumstances. However, those who spare some time for looking ahead — keeping up with housing costs and availability, budgeting their income, and perhaps even applying for a mortgage loan preapproval — will be able to move very quickly when a desirable house comes on the market, or mortgage rates are most favorable.

Train your successor! It is an effective way to apply anticipation. First, it forces you to organize your work efficiently. It encourages those working with you to learn more and expand their horizons. Then, it will open up more opportunities for yourself. Your superiors will know that when they promote or transfer you the work you leave behind will be carried on by others who are well prepared. How often have you heard about someone doing a job so well that he or she could never leave it?

And, finally, anticipation leads to *dynamic initiative,* the skill and aptitude that kept one executive I knew on the cutting edge for forty years. Following World War II he advanced from electronic engineer to chief executive of one of the premier television manufacturers in the United States. As production of televisions in the United States waned, he did not yield passively to this setback. He had prepared himself to transfer his expertise and energies to microchips and computer peripherals, thereby prospering handsomely as an important player in a burgeoning industry.

Good judgment based on knowledge and experience is essential to *initiative* just as it is to the other people-skills necessary to improve positive personal effectiveness. As a principal factor in *initiative,* good judgment often begins with open-minded imagination and an ability to utilize fresh concepts effectively to arrive at a conclusion as to whether, when and what *initiatives* must be taken. At the outset those in a leadership role (parent, coach, manager, chairperson, guide, pastor, teacher, surgeon) must clearly communicate the basic concepts and purpose of the actions to those who may be involved or affected to be sure they understand the wisdom of accepting and the value of following such leadership initiatives.

Energy also is a characteristic of many people who exhibit outstanding *initiative.* Their attitude is marked by intellectual vigor and often physical vitality and stamina as well. To initiate something — whether a project, an idea, or a discussion — requires determination and drive. Being a "self-starter" implies having the power of in-built determination. We owe it to ourselves to do everything possible to maintain and improve our intellectual drive and physical fitness as much as possible so that we can apply that extra effort when we need it.

Action, another element of *initiative,* always should be meaningfully appropriate to the task at hand and not taken just for its own sake. When action is necessary and you believe you know what is best to be done, *don't hesitate.* There are people who may be able to generate good ideas or think of most of the important things that ought to be done, but find it difficult to overcome inertia in translating their thoughts into realistic actions that fit specific situations. Acting promptly as well as sensibly is a crucial factor whenever taking the *initiative.*

Self-confidence in taking responsible timely action grows with experience. The confidence that others place in you will also grow according to your successes.

Follow-through is too often overlooked as an element in *initiative.* It generates the momentum necessary to get the job done. When we initiate anything, we must also work diligently to see it to its successful conclusion. A football analogy would be a successful 85-yard drive down the field, where the quarterback tenaciously keeps moving the ball forward —

repeatedly throwing passes to his teammates for long and short yardages — until they reach the end zone and a touchdown.

To sustain the momentum in any undertaking, follow-through is crucial. Accomplishment often requires unwavering tenacity and, sometimes, great strength of character. Aesop's fable of "The Tortoise and the Hare" teaches us that the hare, who had the natural talent, lost the race because he overconfidently stopped and allowed himself to rest. Don't get side-tracked. Maintaining momentum builds successful careers. This, I have seen happen over and over again. *Loss of momentum can be the graveyard of a promising career!*

Self-Discipline:

Hallmark of
a true leader

*The first and best victory is to
conquer self.*

— PLATO

SELF-DISCIPLINE IS DETERMINATION TEMPERED with
patience. It is indispensable as a guiding moderator in the
appropriate application of our best efforts in the practice of all
of our people-skills. *Self-discipline* is the essence of responsible personal effectiveness.

The ability to exercise suitable restraint over our impulses, emotions and personal preferences is important, often crucial. Sometimes this means patience, waiting until circumstances are more favorable for achieving the desired results in a more positive or acceptable way. At the same time, *self-discipline* also trains us to act or take the *initiative* without hesitation so as to maximize the value of an opportunity or minimize the possibility of unwanted consequences.

Self-discipline is a hallmark of true leadership. It is a characteristic that enables a leader to subordinate personal feelings when serving the best interests of those dependent on the results of a group's efforts.

The experienced leader has a well-developed sense of timing relative to the task at hand and the successful achievement of individual or group goals. This valuable quality helps her or him to decide quickly whether taking immediate action at a particular time would be wise, or possibly premature, and govern his or her actions accordingly. *Self-discipline* also enables an alert leader to stay in a state of readiness to exercise whatever *initiative* may be needed to get the job done.

Often, there are occasions when *self-discipline* will help to make a significant difference in personal relationships. For instance, during a conversation it may become glaringly obvious that you simply cannot accept what someone has just said, or the manner in which it was said. Instinctively you may want to blurt out a vociferous dissent. Instead of impulsively voicing an objection, would it not be more productive to have the patience to probe and try to understand some of the reasons or background behind what, at the moment, seemed so outrageous? Self-disciplined restraint and *tact* might give both sides the opportunity to at least understand, if not accept, each other's point of view.

Making an effort to avoid a counterproductive flat-out confrontation can have a strong interactive effect. This sort of restraint would be as helpful and beneficial in an interchange with your child as in a discussion with your boss. Clearly, a child would respond to and learn a great deal from a parent's example of practiced *self-discipline*.

Focus on the light at the end of the tunnel! Remember this and chances are that you will not panic or "lose your cool" when the going gets rough. Despite your best efforts, you may at times face disappointments and frustrations because of outside events that are beyond your control. Gross misinterpretation or misunderstanding by others of your purpose or actions, or even some serious miscalculation of your own, may precipitate a crisis. Whatever the cause, particularly when in a leadership role, this is no time to panic. On the contrary, this is when *self-discipline* helps you to keep cool and apply your best judgment to ameliorate the situation, or even cut your losses, depending on whatever course is the least damaging.

Looking ahead to the light at the end of the tunnel and the rewards of achieving your goals — a graduation, a promotion, the joys of parenthood, paying off the mortgage — can keep you on track so that you can have the *self-discipline* to stay the course during crucial periods along the way.

Establish priorities. *Self-discipline* implies personal responsibility and respect for others as well as yourself. In today's complex, fast-paced life, some of us, for instance, are sandwiched between helping our aged parents and providing for the needs of our children. We may become terribly stressed by the demands of career, family and our own personal aspirations and obligations. It is essential to try to foresee the problems that could result from overextending our capabilities unrealistically. There will never be a perfect solution, but establishing priorities — short- and long-term — will lead to more realistic commitments which everyone can expect will be implemented successfully. This is where *objectivity* is strongly linked to *self-discipline.*

Timing and timeliness: As you may have already noted, the value of timing and timeliness has been mentioned in earlier chapters of *Improving Personal Effectiveness*. Timeliness is reemphasized here because it is such a vital element in having the *self-discipline* necessary for achieving success in dealings with others. Combining the *what, how* or *why* we do or say anything with a sense of *when,* can heighten our personal effectiveness in achieving desired outcomes. The timeliness factor in *self-discipline* helps to pace, organize and focus our efforts.

The individual with a good sense of timing and *self-discipline* often gains the benefits as well as the enviable reputation of being the right person in the right place at the right time. In 1927 Charles Lindbergh was the first to fly solo non-stop over the Atlantic from New York to Paris. This feat brought him a prize and renown, and opened the door to many opportunities for him.

While many other pilots around the world were still preparing to attempt this flight, Lindbergh took off. Fully aware of his own capabilities, his plane's capacities, and the risks, he recognized his moment and seized it. The world hailed him as "Lucky Lindy." However, more than luck turned an obscure airmail pilot into a national hero. (Some would say that "luck" makes a better word, when you put the letter "p" before it.)

It has been wisely suggested there's a time to lead, a time to follow, and a time to stay out of the way. *Self-discipline* and *adaptability* build our capacity to shift gears effectively as the occasion may require. When good judgment in assessing the appropriate need of the moment is linked to worthy future objectives, full confidence in our leadership is inspired among our associates, our friends, and within our own families.

Developing *self-discipline* requires a high degree of motivation, practice and persistence. It is much easier for us to be impulsive, or give way to impatience, fear, and other pressures. However, each successful outcome of a situation in which we exercise thoughtful restraint reinforces our ability to master ourselves. As a self-disciplined person, equipped with capability in all of the powerful people-skills, each of us can feel more assured that we are better prepared to deal effectively with whatever situation may arise.

Does this sound difficult and daunting? You probably are more self-disciplined than you think. You may not have realized how much of this powerful people-skill you already are exercising, by:

- ✧ Being considerate of others,

- ✧ Keeping your professional and vocational training current, even at the cost of some of your leisure time,

- ✧ Pursuing your career path conscientiously,

- ✧ Keeping fit,

- ✧ Sticking to a personal financial plan,

- ✧ Staying the course despite distractions,

- ✧ Maintaining an even temperament in the face of difficulties,

- ✧ Honoring the Golden Rule.

Part IV.
Looking Ahead

Looking Ahead:

Commitment to excellence

Excellence is won by training.

—ARISTOTLE

SINCE NO TWO SITUATIONS WILL EVER BE QUITE ALIKE, the degree to which any of one of the nine powerful people-skills comes into play will always vary. They are links in a chain, and the more we strengthen one, the stronger the entire chain becomes. Therefore, each should be developed and, like all useful skills, kept sharp and ready to use.

Life in general can be very much like playing the game of golf. The ball and each of the clubs with which we play the game are standardized or designed to fit specific functions. However, the "lie" — or where the ball comes to rest anywhere on the golf course — is never the same.

For example, although a player would use a sand wedge when the ball lands in a sand trap, the actual execution of the shot is never — absolutely *never* — the same. Conditions vary from bunker to bunker. The sand in the bunker may be coarse or soft; it may be dry or damp; the distance the ball must travel to the hole may be short or long, or even over a steep embankment. The ball may be buried or on top of the sand.

To accommodate these variables, in order to get the ball safely out of the trap, the player must make suitable adjustments in the way he or she stands, holds the sand wedge and hits the ball. And, he or she may not be able to do it on the first try! The important lesson here is that this is not the time to quit playing the game. By learning to make appropriate adjustments and by continued practice to improve capabilities, one's level of performance can be raised considerably.

Par is the established goal of most golfers. Better than par is an ideal to shoot for. Although there is only one Jack Nicklaus, the rest of us keep playing the game, and trying to improve. This makes the game a continuing personal challenge and any degree of success we can achieve very rewarding. It is also true in life that if we aim at ideal performance — even though it may not appear to be fully attainable — it is quite certain that we can achieve more than if we had not tried.

Those who have read this far have probably identified their own strong positive people-skills as well as those skills that they may have not thought much about before in the context of personal effectiveness. To maintain the momentum of the process of further improving positive interactive people-skills, build on the *good and work on the wanting.*

Try to make it an ongoing practice to reflect on your day and evaluate the various situations in which you found yourself. Once you get into this habit, you can start to learn from assessing what you and others may have done, or not done, effectively. *When were you most satisfied with the results of an interactive effort? When and how could you have better achieved your goal?*

Excellence in any worthwhile endeavor is achieved by dedication to high standards. Usually, it is more productive to "stretch" a little farther. Commitment and practice should help bring you closer to achieving your goal of *Improving Personal Effectiveness*

> *The mechanic who would perfect his worth*
> *must first sharpen his tools.*

—CONFUCIUS

Part V.

Personal Effectiveness Profile©

Personal Effectiveness Profile:

Tracking your own progress

IN EVERY CHAPTER YOU HAVE BEEN ENCOURAGED to examine how you have applied a particular people-skill in your own experience. For instance, by examining an interpersonal experience retrospectively, you can often learn where and how the outcome might have been improved. *"What could I (or the other person) have thought, said or done differently?"* Now you can ask yourself, *"How am I doing?"*

The Personal Effectiveness Profile© is a further step in the process; providing a convenient aid to periodically evaluate your development and track your progress, skill by skill and in overall performance. It is designed to show you your own assessment of where you may stand at any time relative only to yourself and your individual and total skill level *according to your own perception*. The result is intended to be an ongoing graphic self-portrait of your personal effectiveness in the nine powerful people-skills. It is meant to be an objective self-portrait, emerging from your tough-minded, realistic effort.

As a self-evaluation, this process does not attempt to simulate a standardized scientific measure, precisely calibrated to produce an exact placement of an individual's standing within the population at large or a subgroup for comparative appraisal. The Profile is here for the personal use of an individual interested in self-appraisal. In order to get the most of the benefit in this exercise, try to be as *objective* as possible — as thoughtfully fair to yourself as you would be to anyone else. As you repeat this self-evaluation periodically, you will be able to see an ongoing trend.

Creating your Personal Effectiveness Profile© is a two-step process:

A. A numerical self-evaluation for each people-skill on a scale of 1-10, with a combined total for all (Figure 1).

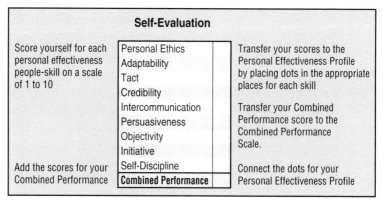

Figure 1.

B. Transferring the scores from the Self-Evaluation to the Personal Effectiveness Profile© and then graphing them.

Personal Effectiveness Profile©

Personal Ethics	Adaptability	Tact	Credibility	Intercommunication	Persuasiveness	Objectivity	Initiative	Self-Discipline	Progressive Development Range	Combined Performance Scale
10 ○	10 ○	10 ○	10 ○	10 ○	10 ○	10 ○	10 ○	10 ○		– 90
9 ○	9 ○	9 ○	9 ○	9 ○	9 ○	9 ○	9 ○	9 ○	SUPERIOR	– 81
8 ○	8 ○	8 ○	8 ○	8 ○	8 ○	8 ○	8 ○	8 ○		– 72
7 ○	7 ○	7 ○	7 ○	7 ○	7 ○	7 ○	7 ○	7 ○		– 63
6 ○	6 ○	6 ○	6 ○	6 ○	6 ○	6 ○	6 ○	6 ○	ABOVE AVERAGE	– 54
5 ○	5 ○	5 ○	5 ○	5 ○	5 ○	5 ○	5 ○	5 ○		– 45
4 ○	4 ○	4 ○	4 ○	4 ○	4 ○	4 ○	4 ○	4 ○	AVERAGE	– 36
3 ○	3 ○	3 ○	3 ○	3 ○	3 ○	3 ○	3 ○	3 ○		– 27
2 ○	2 ○	2 ○	2 ○	2 ○	2 ○	2 ○	2 ○	2 ○		– 18
1 ○	1 ○	1 ○	1 ○	1 ○	1 ○	1 ○	1 ○	1 ○	BELOW AVERAGE	– 9
0 ○	0 ○	0 ○	0 ○	0 ○	0 ○	0 ○	0 ○	0 ○		– 0

Notes _____

_____

_____

Figure 2.

Before attempting to do your own Personal Effectiveness Profile© please study the example of a profile for a hypothetical John Smith on page 102 (Figure 3) and the explanation which follows it. Doing this will help you to get started on your own self-evaluation.

Date _____ 9/1/95 _____

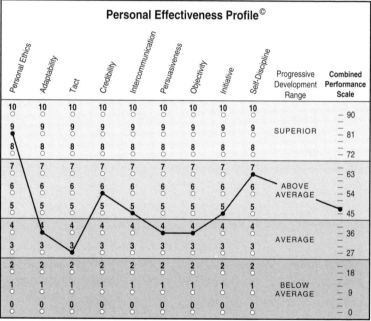

Self-Evaluation

Score yourself for each personal effectiveness people-skill on a scale of 1 to 10	Personal Ethics	9
	Adaptability	4
	Tact	3
	Credibility	6
	Intercommunication	5
	Persuasiveness	4
	Objectivity	4
	Initiative	5
Add the scores for your Combined Performance	Self-Discipline	7
	Combined Performance	47

Transfer your scores to the Personal Effectiveness Profile by placing dots in the appropriate places for each skill

Transfer your Combined Performance score to the Combined Performance Scale.

Connect the dots for your Personal Effectiveness Profile

Personal Effectiveness Profile©

Notes _Review chapters on tact and adaptability._
Re-evaluate in two months.

Figure 3. Personal Effectiveness Profile©, "John Smith."

As you can see, John's total profile shows a picture that is more than just a sum of his individual people-skills. By looking at the horizontal shaded bands, we can quickly see his people-skills strengths and those he will want to review and work on. Significantly, when we follow the line of John's profile to the last column, Combined Performance Scale, it tracks over a Progressive Development Range that is in the Above Average band. Thus, although he gave himself only one score falling in the Superior band, and the others are Above Average or Average, his complete profile clearly indicates that he has a high potential for improving his personal effectiveness.

You may well be encouraged when you see how high you find yourself on the Progressive Development Range of your initial self-profile. This happens often because individuals who are interested in self-improvement already have some of the basics before they get into the serious process of *Improving Personal Effectiveness.* Whether you work on one or more of the skills, it will be both constructive and satisfying to track your progress as you go along.

You will find seven Personal Effectiveness Profile© forms bound in the book so that you can reevaluate yourself periodically, as often as you may decide will be useful to you. You have taken the *initiative;* now try to build and maintain the momentum!

Benjamin Franklin — an icon of self-improvement — tells us that initially he kept a weekly record of his efforts in a paper notebook, and erased his marks so often to keep track of his progress that he soon wore holes in the paper!

Date _____

Personal Effectiveness Profile©

Self-Evaluation

Score yourself for each personal effectiveness people-skill on a scale of 1 to 10	Personal Ethics Adaptability Tact Credibility	Transfer your scores to the Personal Effectiveness Profile by placing dots in the appropriate places for each skill
	Intercommunication Persuasiveness Objectivity Initiative	Transfer your Combined Performance score to the Combined Performance Scale.
Add the scores for your Combined Performance	Self-Discipline **Combined Performance**	Connect the dots for your Personal Effectiveness Profile

Personal Effectiveness Profile©

Personal Ethics	Adaptability	Tact	Credibility	Intercommunication	Persuasiveness	Objectivity	Initiative	Self-Discipline	Progressive Development Range	Combined Performance Scale
10	10	10	10	10	10	10	10	10		– 90
9	9	9	9	9	9	9	9	9	SUPERIOR	– 81
8	8	8	8	8	8	8	8	8		– 72
7	7	7	7	7	7	7	7	7		– 63
6	6	6	6	6	6	6	6	6	ABOVE AVERAGE	– 54
5	5	5	5	5	5	5	5	5		– 45
4	4	4	4	4	4	4	4	4	AVERAGE	– 36
3	3	3	3	3	3	3	3	3		– 27
2	2	2	2	2	2	2	2	2		– 18
1	1	1	1	1	1	1	1	1	BELOW AVERAGE	– 9
0	0	0	0	0	0	0	0	0		– 0

Notes _____

_____

_____

{ 104 }

Personal Effectiveness Profile©

Self-Evaluation

Score yourself for each personal effectiveness people-skill on a scale of 1 to 10

Personal Ethics	
Adaptability	
Tact	
Credibility	
Intercommunication	
Persuasiveness	
Objectivity	
Initiative	
Self-Discipline	
Combined Performance	

Transfer your scores to the Personal Effectiveness Profile by placing dots in the appropriate places for each skill

Transfer your Combined Performance score to the Combined Performance Scale.

Add the scores for your Combined Performance

Connect the dots for your Personal Effectiveness Profile

Personal Effectiveness Profile©

Personal Ethics	Adaptability	Tact	Credibility	Intercommunication	Persuasiveness	Objectivity	Initiative	Self-Discipline	Progressive Development Range	Combined Performance Scale
10	10	10	10	10	10	10	10	10		— 90
9	9	9	9	9	9	9	9	9	SUPERIOR	— 81
8	8	8	8	8	8	8	8	8		— 72
7	7	7	7	7	7	7	7	7		— 63
6	6	6	6	6	6	6	6	6	ABOVE AVERAGE	— 54
5	5	5	5	5	5	5	5	5		— 45
4	4	4	4	4	4	4	4	4	AVERAGE	— 36
3	3	3	3	3	3	3	3	3		— 27
2	2	2	2	2	2	2	2	2		— 18
1	1	1	1	1	1	1	1	1	BELOW AVERAGE	— 9
0	0	0	0	0	0	0	0	0		— 0

Notes _____

_____

_____

Personal Effectiveness Profile©

Self-Evaluation

Score yourself for each personal effectiveness people-skill on a scale of 1 to 10

| Personal Ethics |
| Adaptability |
| Tact |
| Credibility |
| Intercommunication |
| Persuasiveness |
| Objectivity |
| Initiative |
| Self-Discipline |
| **Combined Performance** |

Add the scores for your Combined Performance

Transfer your scores to the Personal Effectiveness Profile by placing dots in the appropriate places for each skill

Transfer your Combined Performance score to the Combined Performance Scale.

Connect the dots for your Personal Effectiveness Profile

Personal Effectiveness Profile©

Personal Ethics	Adaptability	Tact	Credibility	Intercommunication	Persuasiveness	Objectivity	Initiative	Self-Discipline	Progressive Development Range	Combined Performance Scale
10	10	10	10	10	10	10	10	10		— 90
9	9	9	9	9	9	9	9	9	SUPERIOR	— 81
8	8	8	8	8	8	8	8	8		— 72
7	7	7	7	7	7	7	7	7		— 63
6	6	6	6	6	6	6	6	6	ABOVE AVERAGE	— 54
5	5	5	5	5	5	5	5	5		— 45
4	4	4	4	4	4	4	4	4	AVERAGE	— 36
3	3	3	3	3	3	3	3	3		— 27
2	2	2	2	2	2	2	2	2		— 18
1	1	1	1	1	1	1	1	1	BELOW AVERAGE	— 9
0	0	0	0	0	0	0	0	0		— 0

Notes _____

_____

_____

Personal Effectiveness Profile©

Self-Evaluation

Score yourself for each personal effectiveness people-skill on a scale of 1 to 10

Personal Ethics
Adaptability
Tact
Credibility
Intercommunication
Persuasiveness
Objectivity
Initiative
Self-Discipline
Combined Performance

Transfer your scores to the Personal Effectiveness Profile by placing dots in the appropriate places for each skill

Transfer your Combined Performance score to the Combined Performance Scale.

Add the scores for your Combined Performance

Connect the dots for your Personal Effectiveness Profile

Personal Effectiveness Profile©

Personal Ethics	Adaptability	Tact	Credibility	Intercommunication	Persuasiveness	Objectivity	Initiative	Self-Discipline	Progressive Development Range	Combined Performance Scale
10 ○	10 ○	10 ○	10 ○	10 ○	10 ○	10 ○	10 ○	10 ○		– 90
9 ○	9 ○	9 ○	9 ○	9 ○	9 ○	9 ○	9 ○	9 ○	SUPERIOR	– 81
8 ○	8 ○	8 ○	8 ○	8 ○	8 ○	8 ○	8 ○	8 ○		– 72
7 ○	7 ○	7 ○	7 ○	7 ○	7 ○	7 ○	7 ○	7 ○		– 63
6 ○	6 ○	6 ○	6 ○	6 ○	6 ○	6 ○	6 ○	6 ○	ABOVE AVERAGE	– 54
5 ○	5 ○	5 ○	5 ○	5 ○	5 ○	5 ○	5 ○	5 ○		– 45
4 ○	4 ○	4 ○	4 ○	4 ○	4 ○	4 ○	4 ○	4 ○	AVERAGE	– 36
3 ○	3 ○	3 ○	3 ○	3 ○	3 ○	3 ○	3 ○	3 ○		– 27
2 ○	2 ○	2 ○	2 ○	2 ○	2 ○	2 ○	2 ○	2 ○		– 18
1 ○	1 ○	1 ○	1 ○	1 ○	1 ○	1 ○	1 ○	1 ○	BELOW AVERAGE	– 9
0 ○	0 ○	0 ○	0 ○	0 ○	0 ○	0 ○	0 ○	0 ○		– 0

Notes _____

_____

_____

Date _____

Personal Effectiveness Profile©

Self-Evaluation

Score yourself for each personal effectiveness people-skill on a scale of 1 to 10

Personal Ethics	
Adaptability	
Tact	
Credibility	
Intercommunication	
Persuasiveness	
Objectivity	
Initiative	
Self-Discipline	
Combined Performance	

Transfer your scores to the Personal Effectiveness Profile by placing dots in the appropriate places for each skill

Transfer your Combined Performance score to the Combined Performance Scale.

Add the scores for your Combined Performance

Connect the dots for your Personal Effectiveness Profile

Personal Effectiveness Profile©

Personal Ethics	Adaptability	Tact	Credibility	Intercommunication	Persuasiveness	Objectivity	Initiative	Self-Discipline	Progressive Development Range	Combined Performance Scale
10 ○	10 ○	10 ○	10 ○	10 ○	10 ○	10 ○	10 ○	10 ○		− 90
9 ○	9 ○	9 ○	9 ○	9 ○	9 ○	9 ○	9 ○	9 ○	SUPERIOR	− 81
8 ○	8 ○	8 ○	8 ○	8 ○	8 ○	8 ○	8 ○	8 ○		− 72
7 ○	7 ○	7 ○	7 ○	7 ○	7 ○	7 ○	7 ○	7 ○		− 63
6 ○	6 ○	6 ○	6 ○	6 ○	6 ○	6 ○	6 ○	6 ○	ABOVE AVERAGE	− 54
5 ○	5 ○	5 ○	5 ○	5 ○	5 ○	5 ○	5 ○	5 ○		− 45
4 ○	4 ○	4 ○	4 ○	4 ○	4 ○	4 ○	4 ○	4 ○	AVERAGE	− 36
3 ○	3 ○	3 ○	3 ○	3 ○	3 ○	3 ○	3 ○	3 ○		− 27
2 ○	2 ○	2 ○	2 ○	2 ○	2 ○	2 ○	2 ○	2 ○		− 18
1 ○	1 ○	1 ○	1 ○	1 ○	1 ○	1 ○	1 ○	1 ○	BELOW AVERAGE	− 9
0 ○	0 ○	0 ○	0 ○	0 ○	0 ○	0 ○	0 ○	0 ○		− 0

Notes _____

_____

_____

Personal Effectiveness Profile©

Self-Evaluation

Score yourself for each personal effectiveness people-skill on a scale of 1 to 10

Personal Ethics
Adaptability
Tact
Credibility
Intercommunication
Persuasiveness
Objectivity
Initiative
Self-Discipline
Combined Performance

Transfer your scores to the Personal Effectiveness Profile by placing dots in the appropriate places for each skill

Transfer your Combined Performance score to the Combined Performance Scale.

Add the scores for your Combined Performance

Connect the dots for your Personal Effectiveness Profile

Personal Effectiveness Profile©

Personal Ethics	Adaptability	Tact	Credibility	Intercommunication	Persuasiveness	Objectivity	Initiative	Self-Discipline	Progressive Development Range	Combined Performance Scale
10 ○	10 ○	10 ○	10 ○	10 ○	10 ○	10 ○	10 ○	10 ○		— 90
9 ○	9 ○	9 ○	9 ○	9 ○	9 ○	9 ○	9 ○	9 ○	SUPERIOR	— 81
8 ○	8 ○	8 ○	8 ○	8 ○	8 ○	8 ○	8 ○	8 ○		— 72
7 ○	7 ○	7 ○	7 ○	7 ○	7 ○	7 ○	7 ○	7 ○		— 63
6 ○	6 ○	6 ○	6 ○	6 ○	6 ○	6 ○	6 ○	6 ○	ABOVE AVERAGE	— 54
5 ○	5 ○	5 ○	5 ○	5 ○	5 ○	5 ○	5 ○	5 ○		— 45
4 ○	4 ○	4 ○	4 ○	4 ○	4 ○	4 ○	4 ○	4 ○	AVERAGE	— 36
3 ○	3 ○	3 ○	3 ○	3 ○	3 ○	3 ○	3 ○	3 ○		— 27
2 ○	2 ○	2 ○	2 ○	2 ○	2 ○	2 ○	2 ○	2 ○		— 18
1 ○	1 ○	1 ○	1 ○	1 ○	1 ○	1 ○	1 ○	1 ○	BELOW AVERAGE	— 9
0 ○	0 ○	0 ○	0 ○	0 ○	0 ○	0 ○	0 ○	0 ○		— 0

Notes _____

_____

_____

Personal Effectiveness Profile©

Self-Evaluation

Score yourself for each personal effectiveness people-skill on a scale of 1 to 10	Personal Ethics Adaptability Tact Credibility Intercommunication Persuasiveness Objectivity Initiative	Transfer your scores to the Personal Effectiveness Profile by placing dots in the appropriate places for each skill Transfer your Combined Performance score to the Combined Performance Scale.
Add the scores for your Combined Performance	Self-Discipline **Combined Performance**	Connect the dots for your Personal Effectiveness Profile

Personal Effectiveness Profile©

Personal Ethics	Adaptability	Tact	Credibility	Intercommunication	Persuasiveness	Objectivity	Initiative	Self-Discipline	Progressive Development Range	Combined Performance Scale
10 ○	10 ○	10 ○	10 ○	10 ○	10 ○	10 ○	10 ○	10 ○		— 90
9 ○	9 ○	9 ○	9 ○	9 ○	9 ○	9 ○	9 ○	9 ○	SUPERIOR	— 81
8 ○	8 ○	8 ○	8 ○	8 ○	8 ○	8 ○	8 ○	8 ○		— 72
7 ○	7 ○	7 ○	7 ○	7 ○	7 ○	7 ○	7 ○	7 ○		— 63
6 ○	6 ○	6 ○	6 ○	6 ○	6 ○	6 ○	6 ○	6 ○	ABOVE AVERAGE	— 54
5 ○	5 ○	5 ○	5 ○	5 ○	5 ○	5 ○	5 ○	5 ○		— 45
4 ○	4 ○	4 ○	4 ○	4 ○	4 ○	4 ○	4 ○	4 ○	AVERAGE	— 36
3 ○	3 ○	3 ○	3 ○	3 ○	3 ○	3 ○	3 ○	3 ○		— 27
2 ○	2 ○	2 ○	2 ○	2 ○	2 ○	2 ○	2 ○	2 ○		— 18
1 ○	1 ○	1 ○	1 ○	1 ○	1 ○	1 ○	1 ○	1 ○	BELOW AVERAGE	— 9
0 ○	0 ○	0 ○	0 ○	0 ○	0 ○	0 ○	0 ○	0 ○		— 0

Notes _____

_____

_____

Appendix:
Suggested Reading

Suggested Reading:

You are the people you've known and the books you've read

The books that are listed here are just a sample of many that are available today. All of us have personal preferences in the type and style of writing we enjoy. These are a few that I would like to recommend.

Emerson, Ralph Waldo. *Essays* (any edition)
   Emerson's essays are all worthwhile. "Self-Reliance" is a personal favorite; especially encouraging in the area of self-improvement.

Franklin, Benjamin. *Autobiography* (any edition)

The classic example of American self-help and self-improvement, read it and understand why it has been in print for 200 years. Through hard work, setting goals, discipline, and life-long self-education, this disadvantaged boy became one of the most influential, successful men of all time. Franklin's wisdom and sense of humor make it a joy and inspiration to read!

Batten, Joe D. *Tough-minded Leadership.* (New York: Amacom, 1989).

This is a no-nonsense, high-power book for those who aim to be top managers and who have the will, patience and industriousness to seriously work at it.

Bennett, William J. *The Book of Virtues* (New York: Simon & Schuster, 1994).

A wonderful anthology of Bible stories, myths, folklore and wisdom of the ages, with concise introductory essays by the author. Worth having in any library.

Bowen, Catherine Drinker. *Miracle at Philadelphia: The story of the Constitutional Convention, May to September 1787* (Boston: Little, Brown, 1966).

A marvelous study of group dynamics and interactive personal effectiveness, featuring some of the most outstanding and towering personalities of all time. Together they wrote the Constitution of the United States, which, with the Bill of Rights, has been amended only sixteen times in 200 years.

Covey, Stephen R. *The Seven Habits of Highly Effective People: Restoring the Character Ethic* (New York: Fireside, 1989).

A "best seller" since publication, provides insights in self-improvement and powerful personal change through seven "habits." It explores in depth principles of personal leadership organized into seven behavioral attitudes.

McGinnis, Alan Loy. *Confidence: How to Succeed at Being Yourself* (Minneapolis: Augsburg, 1987).

A short, easy-to-follow guide to developing self-confidence by developing one's own attributes more fully and overcoming handicaps.

Robert, Michel. *The Essence of Leadership: Strategy, Innovation, and Decisiveness* (New York, Quorum, 1991).

Here is another set of "fundamentals" of leadership and the dynamics of their application to developing meaningful growth in an organization in a worldwide highly competitive laissez-faire economic society.

Taylor, Robert L., and Rosenbach, William E. *Leadership: Challenges for Today's Manager* (New York: Nichols, 1989).

A well organized selection of 19 articles on challenges for the developing as well as manager-in-place, each by an acknowledged authority. Read especially "Managers Make Their Own Rules," page 191.

Thomas, Lewis. *Late Night Thoughts on Listening to Mahler's Ninth Symphony* (New York: Viking, 1983).

Read the whole book, but especially "Seven Wonders," in which the seventh wonder is about childhood and human language development. Any book by Thomas is worthwhile, for the clarity of thought and the beauty of his language.